THE VERDICT IS IN:

FIX THE CRIMINAL JUSTICE SYSTEM

BY

JASON W. SWINDLE, SR., ESQ.

GEORGIA CRIMINAL DEFENSE ATTORNEY

The Verdict Is In:
Fix the Criminal Justice System

© 2015 Forward by: Michael L. Hubbard, Esq.

Edited by: Kristina M. Jacobs, PhD

Published by: TC Bradley - Cape Coral, Florida

ISBN-13:
978-1518782473

ISBN-10:
1518782477

Printed in the United States of America

First Printing, 2015

DEDICATION

This book is dedicated to Gerald "Gerry" Patrick Word, Sr. and Maryellen Simmons. You believed in me when I could not.

TABLE OF CONTENTS

Chapter Three: Criminal Justice Reform

- *How Incarceration Affects Families*
- *The Addiction-Incarceration Connection*
- *A Second Chance for Convicted Felons*
- *Drug/Mental Health Courts*
- *Marijuana*
- *Fixing the Broken Parts of the Criminal Justice System*
- *The Benefits of DUI Courts*
- *The Death Penalty*
- *The Importance of Fiscal Responsibility*

Chapter Four: Life After a Conviction

- *Employment Rights and Issues for Felons*
- *Gun Rights/Gun Control for Convicted Felons*
- *Voting Rights and Restoration*

Chapter Five: Resources Inside the System

- *Finding a Defense Attorney*
- *Preparing Yourself for Court*
- *Prison Addiction and Recovery Units*
- *AA/NA Groups*
- *Counseling*
- *Pastoral Care*
- *Getting an Education*
- *Gaining Marketable Job Skills*

Chapter Six: A Life of Service

Conclusion

About the Author

FORWARD

Michael L. Hubbard, Esq., a Georgia Criminal Defense Attorney, has seen firsthand how important reforming our criminal justice system is to improving the everyday lives of men, women and children who have been affected by incarceration and crime. He writes:

Very early in my criminal defense practice, Judge Rowland Barnes was appointing me felony cases in downtown Atlanta so that I could earn enough money to pay my rent. In one particular case I represented an elderly man with a crack cocaine addiction. He was charged with what was about his 30th case of illegal possession of crack cocaine. After reviewing the evidence and the lack of any defense, I told him that the District Attorney's offer in the case was a "5 serve 1." This meant 1 year to be served in prison with another 4 years on probation. The response that I received from my client was the beginning of my true legal education. Instead of focusing on Constitutional Theory and the other things I had studied in law school in preparation for the bar exam, I was now getting a real education on how our criminal justice system really works and what I needed to know to be an effective Criminal Defense Attorney in Georgia.

My client, in a very cool and confident manner, told me to tell the District Attorney that he would not accept his offer of 5 serve 1, but that he would accept an offer of 5 serve 2. My puzzled look and scratching of my head was well anticipated by my client. "I'll do less time that way" was his response. What was I missing? Last I checked 2 years is more than 1 year. Showing a surprising amount of patience with his brand new, appointed Criminal Defense Attorney, my client went on to explain that because his felony was a non-violent one, he would be released on parole after serving just under 1/3 of his sentence. Two years is 24 months, and 1/3 of that is eight, so he would be released on parole in just less than eight months, he explained. Of course my response was that that 1 year is 12 months, and 1/3 of that would be four months, which is less than eight months. Again, showing great patience to this state licensed Criminal Defense Attorney and former Prosecutor, my client pointed out that the parole process and paperwork couldn't possibly be completed in four months and that instead would take 7-8 months. He further explained that with limited budgets and man hours, the Parole Board wouldn't even bother with his "short time" case simply to release him a couple of months early, but that the Board would indeed do so to release him early on a longer two year sentence.

I was very nervous and a bit unsure of myself as my client and I approached Judge Barnes to enter into the guilty plea. Instead of me advising my client, it was he that was advising me. I had just gotten schooled by a 67 year old crack cocaine addict. Why was this the first time I had ever heard any of this? Nobody explained this in law school. It certainly wasn't on the bar exam. Nor had I ever been advised to such by my fellow defense attorneys, including those that were serving as my mentor. After Judge Barnes accepted the guilty plea and sentenced my client to 5 serve 2, I shook my client's hand, looked him in the eye, and wished him the best of luck going forward. Then, I did something I thought I would never do; I thanked him for educating me about the system and explaining something to me that I had not even considered before. "Hang in there, you'll get it," was his parting response to me.

In the months and years following that experience, I found myself thinking of that client often. While I don't condone his crack addiction, I can tell you without hesitation that man was an expert when it came to certain, limited issues pertaining to our criminal justice system. He knew the problems that he was facing. He knew his goal. He waded through all of the hysteria, confusion, and misinformation and applied his knowledge and experience to come up with a very original, unique, and non-traditional approach towards reaching his goal. Countless others accepted a 5 serve 1 recommendation that day, but he didn't. He confidently accepted a 5 serve 2. I followed up with his case later, and sure enough, he was released 7 months and 23 days into his 2 year sentence. This would not have been the case had he accepted the original offer of 5 to serve 1.

Many years later I still think of that client and now more than ever I believe our society needs the type of education I received from him all those years ago. It's time for the general public to have our own expert. We need someone that will remove all the legal mumbo jumbo and explain to us the way our criminal justice system actually works in real life. We need someone to cut through the confusion and misinformation and explain the reality of our system. We need this expert to identify the problems plaguing our system as well as some fresh, new, and non-traditional ideas to solve these problems. We don't need red state/blue state rhetoric; nor do we need Prosecution vs. Defense rhetoric; we need unique ideas that make sense no matter the color of your state or the position that you hold. Considering the extreme importance of our criminal justice system,

Now, fellow Georgia Criminal Defense Attorney, Jason W. Swindle, Sr., Esq. has stepped up with his new book *The Verdict Is In: Fix The Criminal Justice System* to embrace non-traditional ideas for making real and lasting change that can and will make a difference in millions of lives nationwide.

Michael L. Hubbard, Esq.

Georgia Criminal Defense Attorney, Douglas County, Georgia

INTRODUCTION

The Criminal Justice system is broken: both the ideal of justice and that of rehabilitation have been lost, but there is hope.

It costs too much, it punishes those with drug problems and mental illness who commit crimes, but doesn't offer them the help that they need, and often, it merely slaps the wrist of violent offenders who go on to offend over and over again. Many prosecutors, defense attorneys, judges and members of the public agree that "the system" isn't working. Until now, there has not been a "boots on the ground" approach to fixing this huge societal problem. This book is the "boots on the ground" approach that is needed.

THE VERDICT IS IN

Georgia Criminal Defense Attorney, Jason W. Swindle, Sr., Esq. has stepped up in *The Verdict Is In: Fix the Criminal Justice System* to offer innovative new ideas and a fresh vision for fixing the broken criminal justice system in an effort to get this important national conversation started and moving in the right direction toward real and lasting solutions. *The Verdict Is In* dares to pull back the curtain of the legal system itself for the uninitiated to see "how it really works in real life."

— **Georgia Criminal Defense Attorney, Jason W. Swindle, Sr., Esq.**

About Jason Swindle, Sr., Esq.

Jason W. Swindle, Sr., Esq. is the Founder and Partner of Swindle Law Group, based in Carrollton, GA, located at 310 Tanner Street. He has been practicing criminal defense for over a decade. The Swindle Law Group currently serves the west Georgia and greater Atlanta metro area.

From 1998 to 2003, Swindle served Word & Simmons, PC as an Intern while in law school and then as an Associate Attorney after passing the bar exam. The firm handled criminal defense cases in the west Georgia area.

In order to get experience prosecuting cases, in 2000, Swindle also served an Internship while he was a third year law student for Peter John Skandalakis, District Attorney for the Coweta Judicial Circuit. Later, he became partner the firm, Drummond & Swindle, PC which primarily focused on criminal defense in the west Georgia area. Swindle stayed with Drummond & Swindle, PC from 2005 to 2012 when he started Swindle Law Group, PC.

He holds an undergraduate degree from Georgia Southern University and a Juris Doctorate degree from Mercer University at the Walter F. George School of Law. Along with his private criminal defense practice, Swindle currently serves as an Adjunct Professor at the University of West Georgia in the Criminology Department. He teaches classes in Criminal Law and Constitutional Law.

For over a decade, Swindle has also served the public by writing a weekly legal/political column and providing legal analysis for television and radio outlets in the west Georgia and metro Atlanta area. Swindle blogs regularly about legal issues and current events at: http://www.swindlelaw.com/2015/.

AV Preeminent Rating from Martindale-Hubbell

Swindle is proud to hold an AV Preeminent Rating from Martindale-Hubbell. The Martindale-Hubbell® Peer Review Ratings™ help buyers of legal services identify, evaluate and select the most appropriate lawyer for a specific task at hand.

National Trial Lawyers Top 100 Lawyers

Swindle has also been named to "The National Trial Lawyers Top 100 Lawyers" for the field of Criminal Defense. Swindle shares, "It is my honor to be included in The National Trial Lawyers' list of the Top 100 Trial Lawyers in the State of Georgia. This distinction represents the opinion of my peers — other trial lawyers in the state — and I certainly appreciate being recognized for my commitment to criminal defense." His firm was also voted "Best Law Firm" in Carroll County in the annual "Reader's Choice Awards."

Named one of Georgia's Top Rated Lawyers of 2014

In 2014, he was named to the list of "Lawyers You Should Know" by the Best Lawyers in America group. Legal Leaders is a publication featuring legal talent across the state of Georgia. In addition to insightful profiles on many top rated attorneys, this publication features articles on current trends in the law. It's a valuable resource in finding top legal talent and making more informed legal decisions." Jason Swindle has also been endorsed for his book by over 100 other attorneys.

Throughout his career, Criminal Defense Attorney Jason W. Swindle, Sr., Esq. has fought for the Constitutional Rights of thousands of citizens. Now, he's taken on the challenge of directing the legal conversation about the reforms needed to make the criminal justice system truly work to rehabilitate offenders and also protect our citizens.

CHAPTER ONE:

CONSERVATIVE VALUES IN ACTION

I am a conservative Criminal Defense Attorney. To many people, it would seem rare that a Criminal Defense Attorney would hold conservative political beliefs. However, you will find that ideas from the right directly address the problems associated with the American Criminal Justice system.

As a Criminal Defense Attorney, I take on every type of legal defense case from minor traffic violations to murder cases and everything in between. Drug cases, violent crimes, sexual offenses, probation violations, warrant hearings—anything that is within the realm of criminal law and criminal prosecutions lies in the area of my law practice. As a Criminal Defense Attorney, that means that I represent people who have been charged, or who are under investigation by law enforcement agencies for violations of criminal laws.

The Importance of Defense and Having a Defense Attorney

If you look at history, many civilizations did not have Defense Attorneys. Human existence over the years has shown many people to have been imprisoned or even executed were actually unjustly accused. Even today, some countries don't allow Criminal Defense Lawyers. If someone is being prosecuted by a state or federal agency, that state or federal agency has not *unlimited*, but *significant* resources in which to prosecute. For somebody to be able to hire, in their mind, the best Criminal Defense Attorney who fits their personality, who fits the case, who primarily, they have trust in, is really one of the most important things that somebody can do when they are charged, or even at risk of being charged with a criminal offense.

It's a very rare case where I would suggest for somebody to go to court on a criminal matter without an attorney, maybe a minor traffic offense, but anything that would be considered a misdemeanor and definitely a felony, they need to have a lawyer and if they cannot afford a lawyer in many cases they have a right to have the court appoint them a lawyer, at no cost to them.

Guilty vs. Innocent

I get asked all the time if I know whether or not my client is guilty and how I can defend people who have committed crimes. The way I see it—I'm not the judge. I don't determine guilt or innocence. Oftentimes when a client comes in, I don't know if they did or did not do it. I can look at the evidence of a case and I can determine the strength or weakness of the evidence and I can come to a conclusion based on that, but my role is to be there as an advocate for my client. More importantly, I'm there to protect my client's Constitutional rights, because if the worst person on Earth who has committed the worst crimes possible isn't protected, then that's a slippery slope, then the next worst person…and the next and then it gets to be where nobody's Constitutional rights are protected.

I don't have a problem at all defending those who may be guilty—in fact, I'm honored to get to protect the Constitutional rights of my clients. There are some clients who come in and hire me who are absolutely innocent of the charges, most of those cases either go to trial, are dismissed or are dealt with in some manner where they are exonerated. There are some clients who are partially at fault or maybe they have been charged with the wrong offense or maybe they have been charged with some offenses that are correct and some offenses that are not correct. Then there are the cases where the police have them "dead to rights" – most of the time when you have somebody who has been caught doing something wrong, they've violated the law, then my position of representation changes in that I'm trying to minimize the consequences for that person rather than trying to "get them off the hook." I think that's where a misrepresentation comes in with Defense Attorneys, where people believe we all try to "get everybody off of everything."

I'd say that the majority of my work is actually about talking and negotiating with Prosecutors about cases. There are discussions, there are disagreements, there are agreements and there are some Prosecutors who are easier to get along with than others, just like people. I might send and receive ten emails from Prosecutors per day about certain aspects of a case. Oftentimes, the Prosecutors are concerned, especially in drug cases, where there isn't really a victim, about figuring out: *How to we help this person not get on drugs again?* Prosecutors are not there to put people in jail, that's not their job. I don't think any Prosecutor that I know believes that's his or her job. It's to seek justice, simply that.

The Role of Conservative Values

As I stated earlier, I have conservative values. My values are both the heart of who I am and what I believe and the basis for how I practice law. I truly believe in the ideal of justice within the law. However, I know the system is broken and I've seen the lives destroyed when justice isn't able to be served for anyone, not for the offender or those that were the victim.

I also don't always fall within traditional "party" lines – I think that's important. I don't think that justice should be a political issue where in order to be heard people need to be either a Democrat or a Republican with no real voice offered to anyone in between, or "other" in their beliefs, such as conservative or libertarian.

So what do conservative values mean to me? There is a group called "Right on Crime" based here in Georgia that shares many of my personal values about the role of the government in our lives and what shape criminal justice reform should take in our nation. Right on Crime is a project of the Texas Public Policy Foundation in cooperation with the American Conservative Union Foundation and the Prison Fellowship.

Right on Crime leaders have created, "The Conservative Case for Reform" outlining their beliefs about the role of government in the criminal justice system. I agree with most of their conservative ideals and have used many of them as the foundation of my suggestions and ideas for criminal justice reform offered later in this book.

The Conservative Case for Reform

(http://rightoncrime.com/the-conservative-case-for-reform/)

The defense of society from internal and external threats is a legitimate public good, and public safety is recognized by virtually all Americans as a legitimate use of government power and funds. Americans must ensure that the government performs its public safety responsibilities effectively and efficiently.

For too long, however, American conservatives have ceded the intellectual ground on criminal justice. Liberal ideas came to occupy the space. They often placed the blame for crime upon society rather than upon individuals. They also failed to effectively monitor many criminal justice programs to determine whether they were truly providing taxpayers with the results commensurate with their cost. Now, the criminal justice arena is starved for conservative solutions for reducing crime, restoring victims, reforming offenders, and lowering costs.

Public Safety

Although crime has declined in recent years, more than 10 million violent and property crimes were reported in

2012. Because government exists to secure liberties that can only be enjoyed to the extent there is public safety, state and local policymakers must make fighting crime their top priority, including utilizing prisons to incapacitate violent offenders and career criminals. Prisons are overused, however, when nonviolent offenders who may be safely supervised in the community are given lengthy sentences. Prisons provide diminishing returns when such offenders emerge more disposed to re-offend than when they entered prison.

Conservatives recognize that there are still far too many victims and too many Americans living in fear in their own homes and neighborhoods. Accordingly, conservatives are united in seeking to use the limited resources in both the law enforcement and corrections systems to maximize further reductions in the crime rate for every taxpayer dollar spent.

Right-Sizing Government

Nearly 1 in every 100 American adults is in prison or jail. When you add in those on probation or parole, almost 1 in 33 adults is under some type of control by the criminal justice system. When Ronald Reagan was president, the total correctional control rate was 1 in every 77 adults. This represents a significant expansion of government power. By reducing excessive sentence lengths and holding nonviolent offenders accountable through prison alternatives, public safety can often be achieved consistent with a legitimate, but more limited, role for government.

Fiscal Discipline

Taxpayers know that public safety is the core function of government, and they are willing to pay what it takes to keep communities safe. In return for their tax dollars, citizens are entitled to a system that works. When governments spend money inefficiently and do not obtain crime reductions commensurate with the amount of money being spent, they do taxpayers a grave disservice. Conservatives must address runaway spending on prisons just as they do with education and health care, subjecting the same level of skepticism and scrutiny to all expenditures of taxpayers' funds.

The prison system now costs states more than $50 billion per year, up from $11 billion in the mid-1980s. It has been the second-fastest growing area of state budgets, trailing only Medicaid, and consumes one in every 14 general fund dollars. Conservatives know that it is possible to cut both crime rates and costly incarceration rates because over the past ten years, seven states have done it: Maryland, Nevada, New Jersey, New York, North Carolina, South Carolina, and Texas.

Victim Support

Punishing criminals and holding them accountable is only part of a government's proper response to crime. Also important is ensuring that crime victims are made whole, treating victims and survivors with respect, making sure they are aware of available services and opportunities for involvement, and reconciling victims with offenders where possible.

In 2008, Texas probationers paid $45 million in restitution to victims, but prisoners paid less than $500,000 in restitution, fines, and fees. Making victims whole must be prioritized when determining appropriate punishments for offenders.

Increasing evidence indicates that there is a genuine benefit to incorporating practices into our criminal justice system that emphasize victim engagement, empowerment, and restitution. These concepts have been demonstrated to yield benefits not only to victims, but also to taxpayers and even to offenders, since an offender fully recognizing and acknowledging the harm they have caused another person is often critical to rehabilitation.

The criminal justice system should be structured to ensure that victims are treated with dignity and respect and with the choice to participate, receive restitution, and even be reconciled with offenders. To this end, the system should ensure that victims are provided opportunities: to obtain notice of all proceedings; to be present at all proceedings; to be heard at every proceeding involving a post-arrest release, delay, plea, sentencing, post-conviction release, or any other proceeding at which a victim's right may be at issue; for reasonable protection from intimidation and harm; for privacy; for information and referral; to apply for victim compensation (for violent crime victims); for speedy proceedings and a prompt and final conclusion; and for restitution.

Personal Responsibility

With some 5 million offenders on probation or parole, it's critical that the corrections system hold these offenders accountable for their actions by holding a job or performing community service, attending required treatment programs, and staying crime- and drug-free. When the system has real teeth, the results can be dramatic: offenders subject to swift, certain and commensurate sanctions for rule violations in Hawaii's HOPE program are less than half as likely to be arrested or fail a drug test.

Government Accountability

More than 40% of released offenders return to prison within three years of release, and in some states, recidivism rates are closer to 60 percent. Right on Crime signatories Newt Gingrich and Mark Earley have asked, "[i]f two-thirds of public school students dropped out, or two-thirds of all bridges built collapsed within three years, would citizens tolerate it?" Corrections funding should be partly linked to outcomes and should implement proven strategies along the spectrum between basic probation and prison.

Reducing recidivism should be a central focus of conservative efforts to reform criminal justice. Conservatives understand that reforming offenders is both a moral imperative and a requirement for public safety. Breaking the cycle of crime and turning lawbreakers into law-abiding citizens is a conservative priority because it advances public safety, the rule of law, and minimizes the number of future victims.

Family Preservation

Incarceration is a significant and necessary factor in public safety, but conservatives understand that there are also other factors. A strategy of vigorous, data-driven law enforcement that results in more crimes being deterred and solved — coupled with effective probation strategies that emphasize restitution, work, and treatment — is essential for protecting communities.

Conservatives know that certain law enforcement techniques enhance safety, others have little effect on safety, and some may actively diminish public safety because law enforcement dollars are being spent inefficiently or in counterproductive ways. Ultimately, the question underlying every tax dollar that is spent on fighting crime ought to be: Is this making the public safer?

According to National Review, "40 percent of low-income men who father a child out of wedlock have already been in jail or prison by the time their first son or daughter is born." The family unit is the foundation of society. In a society in which too many young men are incarcerated, marriage rates are depressed and far too many children grow up in single-parent homes. Instead of harming families, the corrections system must harness the power of charities, faith-based groups, and communities to reform offenders and preserve families.

Free Enterprise

The Constitution lists only three federal crimes, but the number of statutory federal crimes has now swelled to around 4,500. The explosion of non-traditional criminal laws grows government and undermines economic freedom. Criminal law should be reserved for conduct that is blameworthy or threatens public safety, not wielded to regulate non-fraudulent economic activity involving legal products.

My Interview with Governor Deal

—Gov. Nathan Deal (R) (GA), Georgia Criminal Defense Attorney, Jason W. Swindle, Sr., Esq., and Swindle's son, Jason "Jake" W. Swindle Jr., 9

I first started thinking about writing this book after I read "A Case for Conservative Reform" and interviewed Georgia Governor Nathan Deal (R) in June of 2013. During both his terms as Governor, Deal has focused on reforming the criminal justice system in Georgia and has had success in creating real change with an eye to improving the lives of offenders and saving the taxpayers money. I am an admirer of the reforms that Governor Deal has implemented in Georgia and it is my hope that we can build on his reforms and create a bigger, nationwide reform of the criminal justice system as a whole.

Deal became committed to the idea of justice reform and reinvestment on the campaign trail for Governor. "After hearing from a multitude of legislators, citizens and even probationers and parolees, I realized that Georgia citizens were not getting a good return on their taxpayer dollars when it came to adult corrections and juvenile justice. A prison bed costs over $18,000 per year; the entire budget for the Department of Corrections is over $1 billion. Yet the recidivism rate among adult offenders is about 35%. A bed in a secure facility operated by the Department of Juvenile Justice costs $90,000 per year, but the recidivism rate hovers around 50%. That's not good fiscal policy nor is that good public safety policy. Our communities and the state as a whole deserved better," Deal explained.

Governor Deal went on to say, "In 2012, I partnered with the Pew Center on the States to provide technical assistance to the Special Council on Criminal Justice Reform. Pew came to the table with enormous expertise on these issues because of work they had done in other states. The Special Council on Criminal Justice Reform, co-chaired by Judge Mike Boggs of the Georgia Court of Appeals and Thomas Worthy, my Deputy Executive Counsel, included stakeholders that represented all viewpoints and provided a great deal of expertise in their own right. The Council carefully vetted a multitude of ideas, best practices and other suggestions. Some recommendations ultimately made by the Council, which subsequently became law, were similar to those already done by Texas and Ohio. But every recommendation was shaped and tweaked to serve the unique needs of Georgia."

I was interested in Deal's opinion on the value of drug and mental health courts since I have clients enrolled in both and because his son, Judge Jason Deal presides over the drug court in Hall County. I also believe that drug courts save lives and money. Deal wholeheartedly agreed with me that drug courts save lives and taxpayer money. He said, "I have seen it with my own eyes through closely following and watching Jason's efforts (Judge Jason Deal) in his own court. I've spoken at many of his drug court graduations. A systematic and sustainable statewide accountability court system is vital. As a result, my FY2013 and FY2014 budgets both contained approximately $11 million available to create or grow accountability courts around the state. My goal is to have accountability courts available in every judicial district of the state."

According to Governor Deal, these reforms are indeed saving our state money as well. "The data analyses and projections show that that the 2012 reforms (HB 1176) will save the state $264 million over five years. The 2013 reforms (HB 242 and HB 349) are estimated to save the state $85 million over five years. Some of these savings will continue to be reinvested into communities to provide services to the appropriate low-risk nonviolent offenders with the hope that we are giving them the tools to be productive, law-abiding, tax-paying members of society."

At the end of our interview, Governor Deal wanted to make clear his general beliefs about the interaction of government and the criminal justice system. Governor Deal said, "I believe in the conservative values of small government. To that end, the most basic and solemn obligations of your state government is to protect its citizens and educate its children. These reforms sit at the crossroads of those two obligations. A "lock 'em all up and throw away the key" mentality is not making our state safer nor can we afford it. These reforms are good first steps and we will continue to be looking at these topics as long as I am Governor. By identifying the low-risk nonviolent offenders who can be steered away from a life of crime by providing the appropriate services, we can ensure that our finite supply of expensive prison resources is used for those offenders that society can no longer tolerate." As a citizen, voter, and father of two boys, I must say that I could not agree more.

CHAPTER TWO

DEMYSTIFYING THE LEGAL SYSTEM

The primary purpose, the role of the Criminal Justice system is to have a means of settling disputes. It is a means of justice when someone has committed a crime or violated a criminal statute. That is the primary goal.

That's why we have jury trials. That's why we have judges. That's why we have an adversarial system with Defense Attorneys and Prosecutors. In America, we have the fairest, best criminal justice system in the world. However, it is still broken and can be fixed over time.

Making Justice Happen

Let's talk about justice. Justice for one person is sometimes injustice for another. Oftentimes in the criminal justice system you have somebody who wins and somebody who loses. An example would be, a person who is innocent goes to trial and they are found guilty by a jury. That is an injustice and that person loses and the justice system loses under those circumstances as well.

Conversely, if you have a guilty person who goes to trial and they're found not guilty. That is another injustice that happens. You can't have a perfect system. What you can create is the best system that human beings can engage in to bring cases and society and our culture into a position where we have the best chance of obtaining justice in individual cases and our society as a whole.

Understanding the Players in the Courtroom

In a criminal case, the primary person is the defendant. He or she has been charged with a crime against the state or government. Then there are the Prosecutors who represent the state. The Judge and possibly other interested parties who are involved in the case will also be in the courtroom. Additionally, there are the victims of the crime and the Defense Attorney working for the person accused of a crime.

An example of another interested party might an Investigator doing work for the Prosecutor to gather evidence about the crime. Oftentimes, a good Criminal Defense Attorney is going to have their own Private Investigator on his or her side to investigate the case as well. Not every case requires a Private Investigator, but in very serious cases this is important.

The Criminal Defense Attorney has the Judge and potentially, but not always, a Jury to hear their case or "defense". The Victim of the crime may also bring what is called a "Victim's Advocate" to help them deal with being in the courtroom and getting through the arduous process. In Georgia, Victim's Advocates work for the District Attorney's office. They are the people who handle a lot of the emotional aspects of being a victim of a crime. They also assist the District Attorney's office in communicating with victims. (This applies primarily to Felonies in Georgia. The Solicitor General's office prosecutes misdemeanors.)

The Role of the Prosecutor

The role of the Prosecutor within the Criminal Justice System is really rather simple. The role of the Prosecutor is: to see justice. Period. The role of the Prosecutor is not to obtain convictions. It is not to satisfy any political interest, any personal interest, or any other person including the alleged victim.

Sometimes that means trying to send somebody to prison. Other times, it may be giving somebody a second chance. For example, maybe it is a first time offender caught with drugs and the Prosecutor wants to do a pre-trial diversion leading to treatment and community service—*for the Prosecutor that is seeking justice.*

The Role of the Defense

Number one—this goes for Prosecutors too— is to up hold the Constitution of the United States. Secondly, the role of the Criminal Defense Attorney is to represent the person who has been accused of a crime to the best of that lawyer's ability. Their job is not to "get their client off the hook." Their job is not to win is many trials as possible to put a feather in their cap. Their job is to do what is in the best interest of the client in a lawful and ethical manner.

The Role of the Judge

I want to talk a little bit about the role of the Judge in the Criminal Justice as well. Chief Justice John Roberts of the United States Supreme Court one said, as I paraphrase, "the role of the judge is to be the umpire in a baseball game." They call strikes and balls. They are not there to legislate. In other words, Judges are not there to create new law at all. They are there to interpret the law and preside over cases.

They are there to make rulings in. In the appellate courts, they are there to review what happened in a trial and decide if there were mistakes that were made at trial—the appellate courts correct those mistakes.

How much power does the judge have in deciding criminal cases?

First of all, the Jury decides guilty or not guilty. The judge decides the punishment specifically within the guidelines provided by the law. (This is true except in death penalty cases in Georgia.)

The judge has a tremendous amount of power when it comes to evidentiary rulings (what evidence comes in and what evidence doesn't come in). That that can materially affect the outcome of the trial. Every criminal offense has a maximum fine or punishment. Some of them have minimum fines or punishments. Ultimately, the judge has to determine what the fine or punishment will be within those guidelines provided within the law if a defendant is convicted of a crime.

The Criminal Process in a Nutshell

Over the years, I have been asked hundreds of times about the purpose of various steps in the prosecution of a criminal defendant. These questions have been asked by clients, witnesses, alleged victims, jurors, and other lawyers. That covers just about every type of person in society. So, I thought it might be helpful to generally explain the criminal procedural process in Georgia from investigation to disposition.

INVESTIGATION – When a law enforcement agency becomes aware of a potential crime, they will obviously investigate the circumstances. This may include witness interviews, crime scene analysis, forensic analysis, and asking the suspect to come in for an interview. It is almost always unwise to provide a statement to law enforcement during this stage if the suspect is not represented by an attorney. If an attorney is involved, an interview can be beneficial under some very limited circumstances.

ARREST – If an officer believes that there is probable cause (the person probable committed the crime), then he or she can request a judge to sign a warrant for that person's arrest. Once this happens, the suspect becomes a defendant, is arrested, and taken to the local jail.

BOND – Under most circumstances, the defendant will be eligible for an immediate bond. In more serious cases, bond may be denied by the magistrate judge. When this happens, the defendant's attorney should file a motion for bond in superior court and request a hearing.

INDICTMENT – While some criminal cases can be prosecuted by the District Attorney by simply drafting a formal accusation, more serious crimes require that the case be presented to a Grand Jury. The District Attorney and the prosecuting police officer will tell the Grand Jurors about the case. The Grand Jury will either issue a bill of indictment (a formal criminal charge) or decline to prosecute the case based on insufficient evidence. This is called a "no bill".

ARRAIGNMENT – The arraignment hearing is very procedural in nature. The defendant and his lawyer simply appear in court and enter a plea of guilty or not guilty. For practical purposes, the plea at this point is almost always "not guilty". This happens because the defense attorney usually does not have enough information about the evidence in the case to make a responsible recommendation to the client. (Many courts in west Georgia allow the defense attorney to waive arraignment and enter a plea of not guilty by simply filing a motion. This alleviates the need for a court appearance).

CALENDAR CALL – Calendar calls are scheduled before the actual trial date in order for the attorneys to make announcements about the cases to the Judge. The announcements give the Judge some guidance on which cases have motions to be heard, will be trials, pleas, dismissals, dead dockets, continuances, etc.

TRIAL DATE – This term is a little misleading. While there may be 100 cases placed on a "trial calendar", only a very small percentage actually make it to a jury trial. Most cases are disposed of by negotiated pleas, blind pleas (where the Judge makes the decision on a sentence), pretrial diversion, dismissal, dead docket, and many other creative forms of non-jury disposition. However, those small percentages of cases do make it to trial. When that happens, a Jury will evaluate the evidence in the case and render its verdict.

During each of these phases of a prosecution, members of our community can and often will be involved. (Hopefully just as jurors). That is why you see so many people at the courthouse every day, particularly during jury trial weeks.

While this may seem like a lengthy process, our judicial system in Georgia bears the responsibility of dispensing justice in the fairest manner possible. In doing so, our Defense lawyers, Prosecutors, and Judges must be vigilant in protecting the rights of alleged victims and defendants. We must also be ever mindful and grateful of the sacrifice that our citizens make when they leave jobs and families to perform their Constitutional duty to serve as Jurors on criminal cases.

The Five Objectives of Criminal Laws

In addition to understanding the steps in a criminal case, it is important to understand the five objectives of criminal laws. Since the time of ancient civilizations, criminal laws have been distinctive for the uniquely serious potential consequences for failure to abide by the law of a specific culture or region of the world. With the exception of monarch, dictatorial and communist rule, every crime in a society is composed of criminal elements that must be proven by some form of prosecution.

Throughout the ages, humans have created five objectives that are now widely accepted for enforcement of criminal laws:

1. RETRIBUTION– This objective is aimed at satisfying the thirst for revenge, anger, and hate. The idea is that criminals ought to suffer in some way for their crimes. This is also the most widely seen goal today.

Put another way, if a criminal has taken improper

advantage, or inflicted unfair pain upon others, then the criminal law will put the criminal at some unpleasant disadvantage to "balance the scales of justice." People submit to the law to receive the right not to be imprisoned or executed. If people break these laws, they surrender the rights granted to them by the law. Therefore, a murderer may well be executed himself for taking the life of another.

2. DETERRENCE– The objective of deterrence has two sub-parts. Individual deterrence is aimed toward the specific offender. The goal is to impose a sufficient penalty to discourage the offender from criminal behavior. An example would be for a judge to sentence a repeat DUI offender to a few weeks in jail with the hope that he or she will not offend again.

General deterrence aims at society as a whole. By imposing a penalty on those who commit offenses, other individuals are discouraged from committing those offenses. The Romans used crucifixion for this purpose. When onlookers saw a criminal placed on a cross, they would think twice about offending the laws of Rome.

3. INCAPACITATION– This is the most simplistic of the five objectives. Incapacitation is designed to just keep criminals away from society so that the public is protected from their dangerous behavior. This is often achieved through lengthy prison sentences today. However, the death penalty and banishment provisions in a sentence can serve the same purpose.

4. REHABILITATION – Rehabilitation is one of the newer aims in the criminal justice system. This is particularly true in the state of Georgia. This approach tries to transform an offender into a valuable member of society. Its primary goal is to prevent further crimes by treating the underlying issues that may be causing the criminal behavior. The best example is the rehabilitation of drug offenders. Many people commit crimes because they are addicted to drugs. If the offender can be treated for the addiction, oftentimes the criminal behavior ceases to exist.

5. RESTORATION – This goal can really be applied to any of the four above. The idea is to repair any injury inflicted upon the victim by the offender. For example, one who steals $2000 from his neighbor will be required to repay that amount as part of the sentence. Restoration, or restitution as we call it in Georgia, is actually rather closely related to concepts in our civil justice system. Society wants to return the victim to his or her original position before the injury inflicted by the offender.

Societies differ greatly on the value of each of these objectives. The United States has implemented a broad mixture of all five objectives. However, we differ greatly by region. Most Southern and Western states still impose the death penalty in the most heinous cases. Other states have abolished capital punishment and use a very lenient system of parole.

In Georgia, we have a healthy criminal justice system that is improving every year with the help of our governor and General Assembly. We use drug courts, mental health courts, and drug treatment programs to rehabilitate offenders in many cases.

CHAPTER THREE

CRIMINAL JUSTICE REFORM

How Incarceration Affects Families

Incarceration affects real people every day. The effect is negative in almost every circumstance. First, it is obvious that some people are not fit to live in society. Extremely violent criminals, child predators, and those who pose a constant threat to our community must be locked up. For these few folks, there is just no reasonable alternative. However, most people in jails and prisons do not fit into this category. Most inmates, whether they admit it or not, put themselves there by succumbing to their own demons of addiction.

How does this affect people on the outside?

Victims of crimes suffer the most. This suffering varies in degrees based on the nature of the offense. Those who have been victims of thefts and other lesser felony offenses can and do get past the violations of their personal liberty. However, victims of violent or sexual crimes often never fully recover. While therapy and time heals wounds, some people will never be able to live full and happy lives.

While incarcerating this class of criminals for many years can fulfill a victim's sense of justice or even vengeance, the incarceration does not take away the pain.

What about the families of inmates?

Convicted felons leave behind family and friends who oftentimes had nothing to do with the inmate's crimes. As a parent, I cannot image one of my young sons ever going to prison. The thought is almost unbearable. Yet, in Georgia alone, there are thousands of parents who live with this reality every single day. Many of these parents will die before their son or daughter is released from prison.

By far, the most devastating impact is on the children. Many of these children come from a culture of incarceration. They grow up seeing their uncles, brothers, and cousins going to prison. For some kids, it is almost a normal occurrence.

What about when their parents are incarcerated?

This has a chilling effect on almost every facet of a child's life. This includes, but is not limited to the following truths:

1. A father cannot be a father when he is locked away in a remote prison or even in the county jail. There is absolutely no parenting whatsoever. A child with an incarcerated parent is lucky to have another involved parent or other family members who have "stepped up" to raise the child. Sadly, in Georgia, many of these children are in DFCS (Division of Family and Children Services) custody.

2. Taking children to "visit" parents in jail is common. However, I disagree with this practice. It further "normalizes" the situation;

3. A father cannot financially support his children in jail. This is obvious. While many inmates are unemployed,

some are hardworking productive members of society when they are clean and sober. The darkness of addiction envelops many men and women in this category; and

4. Hate and fear develop within many of these children. They will be much more likely to commit crimes themselves, become involved in the juvenile justice system, and eventually go to prison themselves.

Fortunately, Georgia has led the way in instituting non-violent drug offender reforms, promoted drug and mental health courts, and has put some offenders back to work while on parole via earlier release dates. These reforms have helped Georgia positively address the devastating effects of incarceration. It will save our taxpayers millions of dollars and more importantly have a positive impact on the most important people in Georgia, our children. But, we must do more.

The Addiction-Incarceration Connection

There is a strong connection between addiction and incarceration. In my law practice, I have seen this connection in action over and over again. When there is a drug addiction specifically, the offender commits crimes because there addiction is untreated and out of control.

They do not have control over their actions on the influence of drugs and their entire life soon spins out of control and revolves around getting more drugs or getting the next fix. Whether the crime was in the actual purchase of illegal drugs or a related crime, such as theft to get money to buy more drugs, the root cause of the problem is the same: the addiction. Treat the addiction and the crime stops.

Right now, our nation's judicial system is just beginning to realize the true importance of focusing on treating addiction in order to permanently reform repeat drug-related offenders. Some prisons offer addiction treatment programs, while others are far behind the times. What is needed is a nationwide reform recognizing the importance of addiction and mental health treatment before the addict commits a crime, during the court process (e.g. specialized drug and mental health courts), while they serve out their sentence and for there to be transitional treatment once they are released.

Fixing the Broken Parts of the Criminal Justice System

The Criminal Justice system is broken. With time, conservative reforms and effort, we can fix it. Reforms need to come both from changes in the law and from changes in how we handle certain types of criminal activity. Right now, a criminal conviction for anything more than a minor traffic offense can destroy lives, families and the lifelong ability to find employment that earns a living wage. The idea of punishing those that break the law was never to destroy their lives forever, especially for first time and minor offenses, yet in practice this has often been the effect of a criminal conviction of any type on the lives of offenders.

This is especially disturbing because it dismisses the idea of reforming those who commit crimes who are suffering from mental health disease or addiction. Some important areas for reform that must be focused on are: 1) The importance of second chances for first time offenders and certain types of convicted felons; 2) the need for specialized drug and mental health courts focused on getting the offender treatment and help; 3) the changing role of marijuana and the law and how this area might be reformed and 4) the need to do away with the death penalty.

A Second Chance For Convicted Felons

The stigma of being a convicted felon in Georgia is staggering. Convicted felons are shunned by society, lose important rights, and miss out on lucrative job opportunities.

The state of Georgia loses as well when we have a large number of convicted felons. Talented workers are barred from industry which stagnates the economy, increases welfare rolls, and reduces income tax revenue.

There are a number of ways to avoid a felony conviction. Dismissals, reduction to misdemeanors, and pre-trial diversion are common ways to help a person avoid a felony conviction. Another procedure that is used is asking a judge for a client to be sentenced under Georgia's First Offender Act.

Georgia's First Offender Act

Thousands of people have avoided becoming convicted felons by taking advantage of The First Offender Act, sometimes referred to as Georgia's "second chance law." The First Offender Act was first enacted in 1968 and allows certain people charged with their first felony offense to avoid both a conviction and a public record if they successfully complete their sentence.

Under the First Offender Act, a criminal defendant who has not previously been convicted of a felony may plead guilty and be sentenced by the court. While most of these sentences involve probation, a person can actually go to prison and still avail himself of First Offender treatment if the judge is convinced that First Offender is appropriate. Upon completion of the sentence, the defendant "shall be discharged without court adjudication of guilt."

First Offender treatment has a risk associated with it as well. If a person is sentenced as a First Offender and violates the terms of probation, he or she can have their First Offender status revoked and be re-sentenced by the judge up to the maximum for the offenses the defendant pled guilty to. However, many who are eligible for first offender treatment are not informed of such when the case is resolved.

The General Assembly and Governor Nathan Deal made a huge stride in fixing our criminal justice system by passing and signing House Bill 310. House Bill 310 is primarily an overhaul of the state's probation system. The bill also provides for First Offender protections retroactively. Thus, upon approval of the court and the prosecutor, a defendant who would have been eligible for sentencing under the First Offender Act may receive First Offender treatment and have the Georgia Bureau of Investigation modify his or her criminal record. However, the judge maintains discretion whether to grant such petitions on the basis that doing so would be in the best interest of the community. Thus, some convicted felons will have a second chance to have a felony conviction removed from their record.

These new provisions do not apply to serious violent felonies and certain crimes of moral turpitude, specifically, crimes involving children, the elderly, and the disabled. There are many Georgians who may take advantage of this new law. The ideal candidate would be a person who entered a plea to a non-violent felony in the past who was not informed by his or her lawyer about the availability of First Offender treatment. I have seen a number of cases like this.

Georgia's Youthful Offender Act

One of the most sad and difficult types of cases that I handle is when a young man is charged with a serious crime and there is overwhelming evidence to support the charged crime. While there are many options to incarceration, sometimes the prosecutor simply will not agree to anything but a prison sentence. If the crime is serious enough, the judge will not go along with a probated sentence anyway.

Fortunately, there is a rarely used provision in Georgia law that can be quite helpful under these circumstances. It is called the Youthful Offender Act.

In 1971, the General Assembly enacted the Youthful Offender Act which is defined by statute. The Act may be available to defendants who are at least 17 but less than 25 years old at the time of their conviction.

If the person is sentenced under the Act and accepted by the Department of Corrections, the youthful offender will undergo treatment in a secure institution, including training schools, hospitals, farms, facilities, and other institutions. To the extent possible, these options will be used for treatment of offenders who have the potential and desire for rehabilitation.

It is very important to note that the Act provides that the trial judge may only recommend in the sentence that a person be given youthful offender treatment. The sentence of the court is sent to the Department of Corrections with the recommendation. The Department of Corrections determines whether to accept the recommendation of the sentencing judge.

Another important aspect of the Act is that it does not function like Georgia's First Offender Act. When the youthful offender completes his sentence, he will still be a convicted felon. In fact, the Youthful Offender Act only applies to felony cases.

Based on my experience, this is a very good law that should be used in more cases. It also falls right in line with the rehabilitation approach to criminal justice. Those offenders who can be rehabilitated can become tax paying, law-abiding citizens when they return to society.

Since it is a discretionary type of sentence, the Department of Corrections can separate the young people who want a second chance at living a productive life in society and those who simply don't care whether they are in prison or not. This part of the Act saves our resources for those who want to take advantage of the programs provided by the Act.

Drug/Mental Health Courts

While Georgia has made significant progress with "accountability courts" like drug and DUI courts, we are still lagging behind on perhaps the most important type of court; mental health courts.

My experience shows a tremendous need for these types of courts. I have handled numerous criminal cases where the defendant would significantly benefit from participation in a mental health court. In most of those cases, the prosecutor agreed with me.

But, these courts do not just help defendants. With the implementation of a mental health court, each county will eventually save money, decrease the rate of recidivism, decrease the rate of all types of crimes, decrease the number of crime victims, protect law enforcement officers, and treat the core issues that significantly contribute some criminal behavior.

The General Assembly in Georgia has given our counties the power to create mental health courts by enacting O.C.G.A. 15-1-16. Additionally, it is estimated that almost 17% of individuals entering local jails are suffering from some mental illness and half of all jail and state correctional detainees with mental illnesses reported three or more prior convictions.

One county in the west Georgia area recently recognized the need for a mental health court in their county. Court officials in Troup County (LaGrange) say that police get over 100 calls a year relating to those with mental health issues, including disturbance calls where someone arms themselves with a weapon and threatens suicide or other family members.

Mental health court officials in Troup County, studied the mental health courts in other counties before implementing their own mental health court. They found that where there were outpatient treatment resources and that outpatient treatment was significant, there was a reduction in police – offender encounters.

It was time to make the move. Three cities in the county donated seed money to jump start the program. Soon thereafter, the state saw the value in it and took over providing funding for the court. Funding covers all patients' medication and recovery costs as well as drug-screening costs.

They accepted their first client in January 2013 and has since produced successful outcomes every year.

The mental health court admits those who have a mental illness as their primary diagnosis and are consistently through the system and not being treated. It is a 12-18 month program. Many of the participants are struggling with schizophrenia, bipolar disorder and depression. Though the program is for those with mental illnesses.

Participants go through rigorous monitoring where they are drug tested twice a week (alcohol and drugs are oftentimes involved in mental health cases), attend weekly or monthly counseling sessions, have to abide by their medication treatment, and keep all doctor and counseling appointments.

Once a month, the program holds court where a superior court judge administers rewards or sanction according to their month's performance and behavior. Judge Quillian Baldwin put it best when he said, "If we can help them resolve that mental issue, there is a good chance that they won't keep coming back and getting in trouble. If we help any of them, we've done something worthwhile.

Now is the time for other counties in west Georgia to consider implementing mental health courts. Troup County has shown our state that this type of court can be a vital success.

Marijuana

Recently, there have been significant changes in attitudes toward marijuana nationwide. Since 1996, 23 states across the country and the District of Columbia have legalized comprehensive access to medical marijuana. Four states have decriminalized the drug entirely.

However, here in the South, we have largely resisted any mention legalizing marijuana out of fears that it could lead to widespread drug abuse and other social ills. There are also cultural and political opposition to easing up on this drug.

Some lawmakers advocate for clinical trials for a marijuana-derived drug that many say could help treat severe seizure disorders among children. Surprisingly, this year, six Southern states have adopted laws establishing some limited access to marijuana products that have minimal or no tetrahydrocannabinol, or THC, the psychoactive compound in marijuana that makes users feel high. Georgia is one of them.

Recently, another conservative state, Utah, issued its first registration card under its limited medical marijuana program geared toward those with severe epilepsy. Under Utah's program, the marijuana extract known as cannabidiol can only be obtained from other states and with a neurologist's consent. The extract can be administered orally. In Georgia, the key to widespread acceptance has been the advocacy of parents who say their children suffering from severe seizure disorders could benefit from the use of the cannabidiol.

However, over the past 12 years, I would say that about 80% of my criminal cases involved drugs (including alcohol) in some way. Almost all violent crimes are fueled by some type drug use by the defendant (usually alcohol, cocaine, or methamphetamine).When I look back and count the number of violent offenses committed when a person is using marijuana, the number comes to zero.

I consider myself to lean heavily to the right on most political issues. I am also not a marijuana advocate. I do not use marijuana and I don't like the idea of my sons using marijuana. However, marijuana is starting to and should be treated very differently than other drugs. I personally don't think that decriminalization is the answer now for Georgia. But, significant downward departures in potential punishment should be seriously considered.

Benefits of DUI Courts

Another common sense approach to crime recently effected in Georgia are the DUI courts. I was fortunate to get to speak w Senior Assistant Solicitor General, Monique Hooper, of the Douglas County Solicitor's Office about their DUI court. Beginning in April 2013, Douglas County began to operate their DUI court under the supervision of State Court Judge Eddie Barker.

Ms. Hooper says that the Douglas County DUI Court has been a success in three major ways:

First, she believes that the court has had a positive impact on individuals in the community with alcohol related problems. Second, by addressing the core problem with many multiple DUI offenders, alcohol abuse, the roads and citizens of the community are safer. Third, the DUI Court saves the taxpayers money by reducing the time spent housing offenders in jail.

According to Ms. Hooper, DUI Court is a voluntary, post-conviction, treatment-based program for those who have been convicted multiple times for driving while under the influence of alcohol.

The DUI Court program offers enhanced supervision, counseling, and treatment to help participants function in the community with continuing support. The program lasts a minimum of 18 – 24 months, depending on participant's progress.

In general, to be eligible for consideration, applicants must:

1. be charged with their 2nd DUI in 10 years or 3rd or more lifetime;
2. be 17 years of age or older;
3. show an indication of alcohol abuse or dependence;
4. have no prior convictions for violent felonies or current charges (either felony or misdemeanor) involving the use of force against another;
5. have no out-of-state warrants; and
6. have a valid immigration status with no ICE (immigration) holds.

There are also considerable benefits of the program to a person charged with DUI. These include:

1. less jail time;
2. a reduction of fine(s), conditioned upon successful completion of the program;

3. community service credit of 200 hours for successfully completing all phases of the program;
4. affordable treatment and alcohol/drug testing;
5. supervision in meeting license reinstatement requirements; and most importantly
6. support in achieving sobriety.

DUI Court is divided into four phases with each having a minimum duration. During each phase, participants are required to appear before Judge Barker in a courtroom atmosphere for compliance checks, the addressing of any issues, and the occasional relapse of a participant.

The treatment aspect of DUI Court is the primary focus. Each participant accepted into the DUI Court Program is required to attend treatment sessions at the DUI Court treatment facility. Group treatment sessions figure prominently into all phases of the program.

Additionally, participants are required to attend formal support group meetings, such as those offered by Alcoholics Anonymous (AA), Narcotics Anonymous (NA), SMART Recovery and/or other organizations. Participants are also required to find a permanent sponsor, and meet with that person on a regular basis. Since accountability must be front and center, alcohol testing is performed on a random basis. Breath or urine specimens may be required at any time.

Ms. Hooper wanted to make it clear that DUI Court is not simply a "slap on the wrist" for DUI offenders. Punishment is always involved in DUI convictions. As a criminal defense attorney practicing in Douglas Co., I can assure you that she is correct. But, DUI courts are clearly the smart, correct, and most cost effective way to address this form of unlawful conduct.

The Death Penalty

WE NEED TO RETIRE THE DEATH PENALTY. On its face, I am a supporter for capital punishment. It serves justice in some circumstances, and ends the lives of some of the most evil men roaming the face of the Earth. I care very little for the opinion of the international community, which overwhelming frowns upon the death penalty. I also do not agree with "anti-death penalty activists." However, the ultimate criminal sanction has become too problematic to continue to implement. Most of these problems should concern conservatives like me.

Consider the five following problems associated with capital punishment:

1. **Wrongful Executions** – As a conservative, I believe that the government should have a minimal role in our lives. When it comes to executing a human, the State exercises the most intrusive action possible. While this type of governmental intrusiveness would be fine with if the condemned were 100 percent guilty, this has not been the case.

Since the late 1970's, almost 150 men and women have been released from death row nationally. DNA testing has been at the forefront of these corrections of justice. How many people have been executed who were actually innocent over the years?

2. **High Cost To Taxpayers** – This may be the most glaring problem with the death penalty. Death penalty trials have lengthy pre-trial proceedings, require hundreds of hours of work from defense attorneys (who are usually public defenders), and take up a tremendous amount of the trial court's time.

Additionally, the cost of maintaining death row and supervising condemned prisoners is very high. It costs far less to keep an inmate in general population or even special housing units for the rest of his life.

3. **Justice Delayed For Victims** – Death penalty cases last for years, even decades, because of the very lengthy and complicated appeals process. The legal process prior to executions can actually prolong the agony experienced by the victims' families and friends. In capital cases, there is no closure for many years to come.

4. **Inherent Differences In Jurisdictions** – In Georgia, some counties seek death sentences in many cases while other counties never do. A person can murder a victim in one county where the DA will always seek a life sentence. Sometimes, if the same murder, with the same set of facts, were committed in the adjacent county, the DA would seek a death sentence.

Additionally, some counties often lack the funds or prosecutorial experience and expertise to seek a death sentence. This is an arbitrary system of administering the ultimate punishment throughout our state. It lacks consistency, fundamental fairness, and is illogical.

5. **Deterrence Theory Debunked** – One of the major historical theories in support of capital punishment is called deterrence. The theory of deterrence suggests that criminals will not commit heinous crimes in states that impose death sentences because of the fear of execution.

However, scientific studies have consistently failed to demonstrate that executions deter people from committing violent crimes. So, there are some significant problems with our current death penalty system in the United States. There are also solutions. For instance, the General Assembly could change the law in Georgia to require mandatory life without parole sentences for certain crimes, such as malice murder, when the State can prove a number of aggravating circumstances (like the killing of a child, excessive brutality in a case, etc.). It would be wise for us to look for less expensive, fairer, and more logical solutions to the problem of serious violent offenders.

The Importance of Fiscal Responsibility

According to the Right on Crime organization, "The prison system now costs states more than $50 billion per year, up from $11 billion in the mid-1980s. It has been the second-fastest growing area of state budgets, trailing only Medicaid, and consumes one in every 14 general fund dollars." Conservatives emphasize cutting both crime rates and expensive incarceration rates. In past ten years, Nevada, New Jersey, New York, North Carolina, South Carolina, and Texas have been successful at reducing crime while also being fiscally responsible with their budget dollars and reducing incarceration expenses. Conservatives must address spending on prisons in the same way they look at both education and health care spending, looking at the actual results gained from the taxpayer's dollars spent.

I do not believe in reforms just for the sake of reform, one of the most important drivers of reform in the Criminal Justice system is to increase fiscal responsibility, both as a state (in my case, Georgia), but also as a nation.

CHAPTER FOUR

LIFE AFTER A CONVICTION

THE VERDICT IS IN

In recent years, re-entry coalitions or programs have been created all across the country. In general, a re-entry coalition is an organization functioning on a local level that:

1. Assists parolees reintegrate into society;

2. Helps to reduce the recidivism rate (rate of repeat offending) in a community;

3. Helps to maintain public safety;

4. Increases the rate of employment;

5. Creates a larger base of taxpaying citizens;

6. Assists in reducing the amount of child support owed by ex-offenders; and

7. Supports mechanisms for people with substance abuse problems.

Most re-entry coalitions achieve these goals through partnerships with government entities, faith and community-based organizations, private donors and other members of the community.

In general, these organizations use an approach that starts at the point of contact with the criminal justice system and includes an emphasis on education, families, health services, alcohol and other drug treatment, employment, mentorship and housing.
West Georgia is fortunate to have a thriving re-entry program.

On May 11, 2011, an organization officially reorganized in the west Georgia area as the Re-Entry Coalition, Inc. (RECI), and since then, obtained nonprofit status. Their mission, like many others across the nation, is to reintegrate former prisoners into the community, reduce prison recidivism, and improve public safety through addressing the educational, employment, healthcare, housing and family relationship needs of prisoners re-entering society by providing support and connection to needed services in the community after prisoners have been released.

The RECI has been providing their clients with the support they need to transition back into the community. The program is designed to help clients overcome any barrier they may face when they return to the community. Basically, the RECI provides support and contributes to their success in establishing a stable life once they are released.

RECI has been fortunate to have strong support in this area. For example, in the past few years, the Community Foundation of West Georgia has partnered with RECI. To learn more about the Community Foundation of West Georgia, go to: http://www.cfwg.net.

We all benefit when those people who have "paid their debt to society" are assisted as they are released from incarceration. These men and women can get jobs and pay taxes, take care of their own children instead of third parties doing so, and reduce the rate of recidivism. This scenario makes for a safer, more vibrant community that pays less in taxes.

I am a strong believer in self-sufficiency. However, ex-offenders often find themselves in overwhelming situations. Money, children, fines, fees, housing, employment and other obstacles are an immediate concern. Without mechanisms supporting offenders when they are released from prison, offenders are much more likely to go back to old friends and hangouts. This easily leads back to a life of crime and thus the circle of recidivism continues to rotate.

Re-entry coalitions provide a great example of local government, the private sector, and community foundations working together for a common purpose. They are also nonpartisan, commonsense organizations that need to have strong support within communities.

Employment Rights and Issues for Felons

It is a well-known fact that finding employment for felons is more difficult than those without a criminal record. Today, there are a range of positions available in the workforce that will hire an individual even if there is a criminal felony record, though there are also many fields that prohibit hiring those with a criminal record.

Generally, when there is a conviction, if the conviction occurred over five years ago, it is easier to become employed in most positions. Many employers look at both the amount of time that has passed without further convictions and the type of conviction the person has in order to make their hiring decision. That said, it is only one factor in their employment decision, companies will also consider experience, education, current job recommendations and other factors in their decision.

If the conviction has a direct connection to the job or if it poses a reasonable risk, then it becomes more difficult for many companies to justify hiring a felon. For example, sex offenders will not be permitted to work around children.

Felony convictions may prevent offenders from obtaining the following types of jobs: Working as a licensed professional (such as a Nurse, Lawyer, or Teacher).; Working with children, in the health field; in law enforcement or working with firearms or other potentially dangerous devices. Small businesses or those that hire independent contractors (e.g., painters, general laborers and construction workers) are more likely to hire former convicts.

Record Restrictions

One of the biggest problems that some of our citizens face when they are arrested for a crime is the difficulty in obtaining employment. I have spoken with and counseled hundreds of people who have sought to have their records expunged in order to get on with their lives in a normal manner.

Expungements can be difficult to obtain and only a small percentage of people even qualify.

However, with the enactment of HB 1176, effective July 1, 2013, Georgia has mandated a new law replacing the former "expungement" statute. This law seems to do away with the term "expungement" and the process altogether. In its place, OCGA 35-3-37 focuses on restricting the criminal history information on people who are eligible. Under the statute, the term "restrict" means that the information will be available only to judicial officers and criminal justice agencies for law enforcement or criminal investigative purposes or to criminal justice agencies for purposes of employment in accordance with procedures established by the agency and shall not be disclosed or otherwise made available to any private persons or businesses. This law has been a huge benefit to thousands of Georgians looking for employment in 2013.

Under the old law, an individual had to petition or take some other action to obtain an expungement. Under the new law, The Georgia Crime Information Center (GCIC) is responsible for restricting criminal records under the appropriate circumstances. While this new law is lengthy and full of exceptions, the three main provisions that the public may be most interested in include the following:

(1) In general, if a case is never indicted or accused, and never referred to the prosecutor by the arresting agency, the arresting agency shall contact GCIC and inform them that the record

should be restricted. There are remedies if this is not done properly;

(2) After an indictment or accusation, GCIC shall restrict the record if: the case is dismissed, the offender was sentenced under the conditional discharge act (the first offender provision for drug cases), and successfully completed the terms and conditions, or the individual successfully completed drug court treatment or a mental health court treatment program (there are some significant exceptions to this provision); and

(3) If a person's case has been on the dead docket for more than 12 months, the person may request that GCIC restrict information regarding that case as well.

It is also important to note that record restriction shall not be appropriate if the individual was convicted of certain sexual and other serious offenses listed in the statute.

It is vitally important for those accused of crimes to go over this law with their Criminal Defense Attorney before making a decision regarding the resolution of the criminal case. The future consequences can have an enormous impact.

This law provides hope for more citizens in Georgia laboring under the stigma of being labeled a criminal. When we have more people working, we have more people taking care of their families, staying out of trouble, in less need of government services, and paying state income taxes.

Gun Rights/Gun Control for Convicted Felons

In Georgia, as in most other states, convicted felons cannot possess firearms. On its face, this seems like responsible public policy. However, this broadly written law only partly addresses the logic for its passage; convicted felons are dangerous criminals prone to violence.

For the most part, this is true. Many convicted felons have committed serious violent offenses in Georgia. People convicted of crimes like armed robbery and malice murder are simply not suited for gun ownership for obvious reasons.

Additionally, gun violence is a serious problem. This is particularly true with the rise in gang activity in the west Georgia area. However, laws should be written with a purpose that does not violate our embedded natural rights. Gun ownership is one of these natural rights codified in the 2nd Amendment.

One of our local judges recently explained in open court the reasoning behind Georgia's Possession of a Firearm by a Convicted Felon criminal law. To paraphrase, he said that in order to protect the community from violence, this law is intended to deter people with a history of violence from possessing guns. This judge hit the mark.

But, should convicted non-violent felons be allowed to own a gun? This question has found itself on the national stage and will likely be an issue in the 2016 Presidential election.

In 2014, Kentucky Senator Rand Paul, called for the restoration of voting rights for some non-violent felons. This idea has caught on with both parties. However, voting rights legislation will never succeed without some of these folks getting back their right to own guns as well.

The right to own a firearm is not like the privilege to possess a driver's license. It is, like the right to vote, is a fundamental civil right. People convicted of non-violent felonies should not have a Constitutional right removed just because of the stigma associated with a felony conviction.

There are thousands of examples of people who have been convicted of forgery, theft and many other non-violent offenses. The vast majority of those cases did not even involve a gun. While these are criminal acts and should not be tolerated, the offender does not put our community at risk by keeping a handgun at home for personal protection.

Why should an 18 year old man, who was caught with more than 1 ounce of marijuana, not be able to take a future child deer hunting, purchase a shotgun for sport shooting, or receive his father's gun collection in a will?

How does taking away their 2nd Amendment right make society safer? It doesn't.

As this idea of decriminalizing gun ownership for some felons gains further support, the question then becomes who qualifies and who does not.

A simple idea would be for the General Assembly to pass a statute that just lists the offenses in Georgia that are considered "non-violent." This probably should be a short list. However, our Founding Fathers would be proud of us for conforming our laws to the very document that so much blood has been given; the United States Constitution.

Voting Rights and Restoration

Rand Paul, is also championing the restoration of voting rights to felons and wants to ease sentencing of nonviolent drug offenders. He wants to downgrade some non-violent drug crimes from felonies to misdemeanors to make it easier for those offenders to get jobs when they get out of jail. I believe that Rand Paul is dead on correct regarding both of these issues.

The voting rights issue is logical. This is a constitutional republic. The only way for this country to properly operate is to have a population with a robust history of voting for the men and women who represent them in Washington, the states, and locally.

My only concern regarding the voting rights issue is the lack of understanding that some people have about the meaning and importance of the Constitution. Perhaps a stronger Constitutional educational approach at younger ages would help to address this problem.

Felony convictions currently prevent people from voting in many states. Felonies range from murder to possessing more than an ounce of marijuana. I can understand the view that people convicted of some serious violent felonies should not be able to vote. However, it makes no sense to prevent a person who was convicted of possessing a small amount of cocaine from ever voting again in their lifetime until their voting rights are restored by law.

The primary purpose of our criminal justice system is to punish people when they commit a crime. When a person has completed a prison or probation sentence, they have "paid their debt to society." Why should they be prevented from exercising the most basic and fundamental right that we have as Americans for the rest of their lives?

CHAPTER FIVE

RESOURCES INSIDE THE SYSTEM

Finding a Defense Attorney

Over the years, I have learned about the importance of choosing the right lawyer for the right case. The beginning of the lawyer/client relationship sets the tone for the entirety of the case. First, I want to point out that not every client and lawyer will be a good fit. The reasons are too numerous to list, but it seems that the personality of the parties may be the most important aspect of problems with attorney/client relationships.

I have found the following considerations to be very helpful:

1. Turn To Those You Trust – The vast majority of my clients became a client because they were specifically referred by another attorney, former client, or someone else in the community. In these situations, the client asked their friends and/or family about who would be the lawyer to turn to.

2. Research – There are really only two ways to get the background on a lawyer. The first is to simply make an appointment and conduct an "interview." You may even want to interview multiple lawyers to see who you feel most comfortable with. Second, you can perform some Internet research. This is fairly easy to do by simply doing a Google search on the lawyer or lawyers who you are interested in knowing more about. By doing an Internet search on a lawyer, you can find out about their background, disciplinary history, website, former client reviews, and much more. Obviously, not everything on the Internet is true, however, there are many reputable legal websites that provide information on attorneys. Some of these include, but are not limited to: http://www.lawyers.com, http://www.avvo.com, http://www.findlaw.com and http://www.martindale.com.

3. Reputation – While this aspect of finding a lawyer is similar to talking with trusted friends and family, it is probably wise to ask about a lawyer's general reputation in the community. Some questions may be: *How has the lawyer treated prior clients? Is the lawyer considered trustworthy in the community? Does the lawyer behave in a professional manner? Does the lawyer have the respect of his or her colleagues and the judges who the lawyer appears before?*

4. Trust – I saved this for last because it is by far the most important aspect of the attorney client relationship. Every time I have a potential client enter my office and ask me to represent him or her, I suggest that the client to do one thing. Make sure that you are choosing the lawyer that you truly trust. Whether that is me or someone else, I always ask them to choose the person they are most comfortable with. I would much rather see a person who is in need of legal services hire someone else if they are more comfortable with another lawyer. The level of trust and cooperation during a legal case will have a direct impact on the results of the case. Disaster is inevitable when trust is either non-existent or broken during the pendency of the litigation.

Preparing Yourself for Court

Over the years, I have learned that some of the "little things" can make a bigger impact on a case than you might expect. One of those "little things" is simply preparing yourself for a court appearance.

Whether you are a client, witness, or have some other business before a court, there is a level of preparedness that a person needs to achieve.

PERSONAL APPEARANCE – Since most people who attend court are clients, this is probably the most important and easiest aspect of court preparedness. Clients usually rely on their attorneys to speak on their behalf. Most of the time, they are only seen in court.

However, the fact that you are being seen in court is important too. To illustrate by example, I once had a marijuana case in Heard County Superior Court before Judge Keeble. I had worked out a deal with the prosecutor whereby my client would not have a drug conviction. As the 9:00 hour settled in, my client strolled into court with a pair of torn blue jeans and a tee shirt. My eyes popped out as I noticed that my client also had a very large picture of a marijuana "blunt", or plant right in the middle of the front of his tee shirt. I was grateful that I was able to catch him in the back of the courtroom and suggest some clothing alternatives. He returned 15 minutes later and was appropriately dressed.

I know that is an extreme example. However, you would be surprised by what some people choose to wear to court. I suggest to all of my clients and witnesses that I would like for them to dress as if they were on their way to Sunday school. This could be a suit, golf shirt and slacks, or a button down collared shirt. I suggest that my female clients simply wear a conservative outfit such as a dress. For those folks that live a "dressed down" lifestyle, that is completely fine. You just need one outfit that is appropriate for court.

BE MENTALLY PREPARED – Some court appearances are routine, dull, and inconvenient to all parties. But, there are some that can have a vital importance to your case. Hopefully, your lawyer will be prepared for the court dates that will impact your case.

Before you go to court, at least touch base with your lawyer regarding what to expect. You may need to look at your prior testimony, statements (if you are a witness), or be prepared to address the judge or the prosecuting attorney in some cases. Knowing the facts of the case can make a huge difference in the outcome.

BE ON TIME – This would seem to be obvious. But, I have seen hundreds of people show up late for court. This shows disrespect for the judge, puts your lawyer in a difficult situation, and can result in the issuance of a bench warrant. If a true emergency comes up, like an emergency room visit, then you need to get the appropriate paperwork to your lawyer as soon as possible. Oftentimes, proper documentation will clear up issues of being late or failing to show up for court.

These are just some common sense ideas to make you more successful in court. They are easy to follow and will have a positive impact on your case whether it is criminal or civil.

Prison Addiction and Recovery Units

Prison addiction and recovery units are a specialized area or type of prison, often different from the general prison population, where offenders are offered additional support and education regarding drugs and alcohol and all types of addiction. They are also housed with others with the same types of problems. Participation and assignment to these types of units is voluntary and usually requested by the offender asking for help in getting off and staying off drugs or alcohol.

These units are staffed by those with specialized training in dealing with addiction and recovery. The idea behind offering this type of specialized programming within the prison system is that many crimes are committed because the offender is addicted to drugs or alcohol and that treating the addiction will also make it so that the person is far less likely to reoffend upon release or return to drugs and alcohol.

AA/NA Groups

Almost all prisons today have recognized the importance of offering support, counseling and treatment (sometimes in the form of well-respected and well researched 12-stop programs) for alcohol and substance abuse. Alcoholics Anonymous (also known commonly as AA) is a 12-step program that is offered in many prisons for those that recognize that they have a problem with alcohol. Narcotics Anonymous (also known commonly as NA) is a 12-step program, similar to AA, for those that recognize that they have a problem with either prescription or illegal drugs.

There are also specialized groups for those who do not have a drug or alcohol addiction themselves but were raised by or live with those that do suffer from drug or alcohol addiction such as (Al Anon). Some prisons offer programs for other types of addiction as well such as Gambler's Anonymous (GA), Overeaters Anonymous (OA) and Co-dependents Anonymous (CoDa).

In these types of recovery-based groups, offenders can meet with professional counselors, but also get a sponsor in the form of someone who is already drug and alcohol free, but has previously suffered with drug or alcohol addiction to provide them support. They can meet with others who share the same issue to talk about their struggles and discuss planning for how to best handle everyday situations where they may be tempted to use or take a drink. In prison recovery groups, there is a strong focus on how to handle the temptations and pressures of returning to the home environment (and friends) upon release.

Counseling

The availability of counseling resources in prison is key. Right now, there are many offenders who are incarcerated that are suffering from significant and often untreated mental illness or drug addiction. More psychiatrists are needed in prisons to find and manage medicine for mental illness that could potentially stop the offender from committing crimes in the first place, if only they have appropriate medical treatment to manage the symptoms of mental illness. Psychologists are needed to help counsel offenders in dealing with their past and their offense, but also in dealing with their time in prison and preparing to adjust to society when they are released.

Peer counseling and group support is another important form of counseling in prisons. The stories of those who have left prison and transitioned successfully back into society are particularly powerful and provide hope to those still inside serving out their sentence. Some groups meet specifically to deal with issues offenders face while serving their sentence such as learning to deal with anger to stop fighting, or gaining the skills needed to resolve problems without verbal threats of violence.

Pastoral Care

THE VERDICT IS IN

Over the years, I have also noticed a number of organizations going into jails and prisons for various reasons. One of the most important and powerful groups is the variety of prison ministries who take the message of faith to inmates.

These groups of selfless believers represent many types of denominations and faiths. I am most familiar with the Christian groups who bring the Word to local jails and prisons in the west Georgia area because I am a Methodist. Most of the men and women who do this service work do not want to be mentioned or given any recognition. They provide ministry to inmates because Jesus advocated this type action.

Over 2000 years ago, before Jesus commissioned all of His disciples to make disciples of all nations, he commissioned a number of John the Baptist's followers to carry on a prison ministry to their teacher. They were to answer the question whether Jesus was the Promised One or whether they should expect someone else.

With the commission went the message: "Go back and report to John what you have seen and heard: The blind receive sight, the lame walk, those who have leprosy are cured, the deaf hear, the dead are raised, and the good news is preached to the poor. Blessed is the man who does not fall away on account of me (Luke 7:18-23)." In that message there was, and is, also "freedom for the prisoners (Luke 4:18)."

While most prison ministries are conducted by Christians who are not incarcerated, the Bible speaks of the importance of ministry within the walls of confinement. Perhaps the most well-known prison ministry conducted by a prisoner was that of the Paul. Paul, who wrote most of the New Testament, was imprisoned and under a sentence of death. Notwithstanding his situation, he was filled with the Holy Spirit, ministered to other inmates and guards, and wrote some of the most important letters in the Bible.

Acts 16:25 also records a prison ministry carried on by prisoners: "About midnight Paul and Silas were praying and singing hymns to God, and the other prisoners were listening to them." That event in Philippi also marked the first occasion, but not the last, when a prison official was also converted by the gospel preached in prison: "He and all his family were baptized... He was filled with joy because he had come to believe in God—he and his whole family (Acts 16:33)."

Based on my experience, I have also seen many inmates "find God" while they are incarcerated. Some of these people used religion or perceived spirituality as a vehicle to try to get out of jail or receive a lighter sentence. These folks are easily identified by most judges and prosecutors. The fake "finding religion" does not work very well when planning a way to responsibly handle a criminal case.

However, the Word of God does have a positive impact on many prisoners and inmates who receive the Word in a genuine way. Oftentimes, a trip to the county jail is the first time a person has ever heard or read the Bible.

While it would be impossible to determine a prison ministry's impact on the rate of recidivism, I can personally testify that I have seen many of my clients change their lives for the better by receiving Jesus Christ as their Savior. Prison ministry does help individuals and society as a whole.

Getting an Education

In 2013, *U.S. News & World Report* ran a story on inmate education stating that, inmates in educational and vocational programs are less likely to return to prison and more likely to find a job once they are released"(http://www.usnews.com/news/articles/2013/08/22/report-prison-education-programs-could-save-money). According to the article, researchers at the RAND Corporation found that inmates who participated in correctional education programs had a 43 percent lower chance of returning to prison. They also found that, if prisoners participated in academic and/or vocational education programs, chances of employment after release were 13 percent higher than those who chose not to participate in any educational opportunities. Department of Justice statistics show that 700,000 people leave federal and state prisons each year and almost 50 percent return to prison within three years.

The cost of providing educational and vocational learning to prisons is much less long term than the cost of housing repeat offenders, not to mention the ultimate cost to families and to our society when offenders return to crime and to prison because they were not able to find a job to survive and support their families. As of 2013, prison educational programs cost about $1,400 to $1,744 per inmate each year. According to the research by RAND Corporation, providing these types of programs and successfully reducing the recidivism rate can save prisons between $8,700 and $9,700 per inmate (based on the cost of housing the inmate if they return to prison).

Gaining Marketable Job Skills

Vocational, Career or Technical education opportunities, specifically, offer a road to skilled employment that pays a living wage in areas that are more likely to hire those with a criminal record. Vocational programs such as food preparation, welding, automotive repair, construction and building maintenance can teach valuable work skills that the offender can use to get a job upon release. Research has shown that having a job is a strong predictor of whether or not an offender will reoffend and return to prison. Those with steady work are less likely to reoffend.

Rand Corporation researchers report that vocational education is most commonly offered in various trade industries, including "barbering, building maintenance, carpentry, electrical trades, painting, plumbing, food service/culinary arts, horticulture, custodial maintenance, upholstery, auto detailing, masonry, welding, and heating, ventilation, and air conditioning."

Some prisons also offer the opportunity to earn industry certifications such as a certification in Microsoft Office, general computer skills, construction, occupational safety, plumbing or electrical apprenticeships, automotive service and welding. These types of certifications and apprenticeships can help the offender obtain employment after release.

It should be noted that many of the common educational, vocational and career programs are in trades dominated by men. For female offenders, there are occasionally different types of programs offered in trades where women are more commonly employed such as: sewing and clothing design, food preparation, cleaning, library work, general office and secretarial work, laundry, childcare, hairdressing; and agriculture. There is a need to focus on providing more vocational and career programs for women in the future.

CHAPTER SIX

A LIFE OF SERVICE

Honoring Our Police Officers

THE VERDICT IS IN

The criminal justice system's foundation is laid by the work of police officers. Their "boots on the ground" provide for the first steps in a criminal prosecution. Some people probably think that it is ironic that a Criminal Defense Attorney would be defending the work of police officers in general. However, I am a citizen of this community first and a Criminal Defense Attorney second. My law practice provides me with firsthand knowledge of the important and dangerous work that law enforcement officers perform in our community and I truly support everything that they do to keep us safe.

First, let me make this clear. My job is to represent my clients, who are charged with crimes, to the absolute best of my ability. Part of my job is challenging police officers in court during cross-examination, motions hearings and trials. Almost every officer whom I have met under these circumstances understands and appreciates that I have a job to do just as they do. Additionally, there are countless times that I can recall when an officer has assisted me during the prosecution of a case by taking part in the negotiation process with Prosecutors.

In my world view, there are two classifications of citizens who in general deserve an extraordinary level of respect. These are military personnel, including veterans, and civilian police officers. Our soldiers have the support of most of our nation. However, law enforcement officers have come under more and more scrutiny as our society "progresses."

Imagine a scenario where we did not have civilian police officers patrolling the streets, investigating crimes, and assisting the public. The community would develop into a violent storm of unimaginable criminal activity. You would not be safe in your home at night, on the road as you travel with your family, or safe from violent attacks by people seeking old-fashioned retribution. Think of "Tombstone Justice" and the lawless west of the 1800's and imagine living that way today.

For most of us, this is unimaginable. But, "civilized human beings" can easily and quickly transform into lawless criminals just trying to survive. This is what life would be like without people willing to serve as police officers to keep law and order, especially in times of turmoil in communities.

Lastly, I am enamored by the courage and sacrifice that our local officers exhibit. Each traffic stop can either be routine or, in rare cases, escalate into a dangerous situation. You never know what might happen when an officer knocks on the window of a vehicle during a traffic stop. Officers have been killed in recent years during such encounters.

Additionally, each search warrant that is executed at a home that may be harboring people who do not want to be found – these activities can also either be routine or become a very dangerous situation for all involved.

The point is that these folks put their lives on the line for each of us in the community on a daily basis. They are also frequently criticized for decisions that have to be made in a split second. This is unacceptable. Yes, there are bad men and women who wear the uniform. There are also bad lawyers, judges, probation officers and others within the judicial system. These are very rare cases indeed. Anyone, law enforcement officers or otherwise who breaks the law, violates the civil liberties of others, or behaves in an unethical manner, shall always be held accountable.

Fight For Our Police Officers

Over the last few years, our law enforcement community has been increasingly under siege from the national media, special interest groups and others who would prefer lawlessness over law and order.

We have all seen widespread coverage of these incidents. However, the coverage of these few isolated criminal acts suggests that police misconduct is a huge problem throughout the country. This is simply not true. Because of my job, I interact with law enforcement officers in numerous counties on a one on one basis almost every day. I am also often in a position where I am challenging their actions, investigations, and judgment. Thorough cross-examination in a criminal case does not lead to questioning the integrity of these folks. My experience has lead me to the following conclusions about the men and women of our law enforcement community:

1. They possess great courage. Officers put their lives on the line every day. A routine traffic stop can and has turned into a deadly encounter for many patrol officers over the past number of years. With the current protests and threats, their lives are more in danger than ever before;

2. They sacrifice financially. You do not get rich by choosing to pursue a career in Criminal Justice. Many of these officers work "side jobs," become business owners, and operate within a tight budget. This is a profession that people choose because they feel the calling to serve the community;

3. They keep us safe. This is the core reason why we even have a police force. Without police officers, our community would become a lawless society where vigilante justice and rampant crime would be the norm;

4. They are honest. As with any line of work, there are dishonest police officers. However, the myth that many officers "plant evidence," lie in court, and arrest people based on their skin color is just that, a myth;

5. When challenging a criminal case, good attorneys will cross-examine officers on what they did, did not do, and what they should have done. These questions all surround the strength or weakness of the criminal investigation, not the character of the police officer; and

6. They are more involved in community service than many sections of society. Organizations, like the Fraternal Order of Police (FOP), are often involved in anti-drug campaigns, victim's rights events, and other charitable endeavors.

We, as a community, can help our officers "fight back" against this tide of unfounded criticism and violence. Show your unwavering support for the people who keep us safe by speaking out against these "protesters," open your checkbook and give money to pro-law enforcement organizations, support politicians who are committed to protecting police officers, encourage top notch young people to consider a career in Criminal Justice, and simply tell the next police officer who you see that you are on his or her side. Lastly, show your gratitude by thanking an officer for his or her service to our community.

CONCLUSION

The Verdict Is In: Fix the Criminal Justice System has outlined innovative new ideas and a fresh vision for fixing the broken criminal justice system in an effort to get this important national conversation moving in a new direction to solve the problems that have plagued our nation for generations. Now, it is up to you to continue the conversation, add your voice and ideas and give power to the call for change so that we can create a new criminal justice system that better serves all people.

ABOUT THE AUTHOR

Jason W. Swindle, Sr., Esq. is the Founder and Partner of Swindle Law Group, based in Carrollton, GA, located at 310 Tanner Street. He has been practicing criminal defense for over

a decade. The Swindle Law Group currently serves the west Georgia and greater Atlanta metro area.

Swindle holds an undergraduate degree from Georgia Southern University and a law degree from Mercer University at the Walter F. George School of Law. Along with operating his private Criminal Defense practice, Swindle currently serves as an Adjunct Professor at the University of West Georgia in the Criminology department. He teaches classes in Criminal Law and Constitutional Law. He is also a syndicated legal columnist and serves as a legal analyst/commentator.

Swindle blogs regularly about legal issues and current events at: http://www.swindlelaw.com/2015/. For more information about Swindle Law Group visit: http://www.swindlelaw.com. Or, download the Swindle Law Group App online from iTunes at: https://itunes.apple.com/us/app/swindle-law-group-p.c./id1022442588?ls=1&mt=8.

46443584R00056

Made in the USA
Lexington, KY
04 November 2015